Home Economics

for

Home Schoolers

(Once-A-Week Curriculum)

Level One

From Pearables

This book is dedicated to all the future mothers and homemakers of tomorrow.

PEARABLES
P.O. Box 1071
Mukilteo, WA 98275

www.pearables.com

Instructions

Dearest Parent in Christ,

After much prayer and study, we are happy to be able to provide a home economics program for the believer in Christ.

While many children are being educated in a variety of academics, many parents are forgetting that these children will also grow up to be mothers and homemakers. Just as it is important to prepare a child in academics (reading, writing and arithmetic), so must we prepare them in household skills in order for them to be able to take care of their own homes and families one day.

We pray that this material will be an encouragement to you as you start on your journey in preparing them in the area of homemaking! We've tried to make it as easy as possible for a child to be able to complete without too much help from the parent.

The following suggestions may help:

1. This is a weekly lesson plan, which means that each project is to be completed within a week.

2. For this book, we suggest that mother set aside one hour each week to work with her child. The curriculum is simple and easy to use, and all it requires is a little time and dedication to learn the skills that each lesson will teach.

3. Once the child has completed a project (for example, making biscuits) have them try this new skill a few more times, all on their own throughout the week, until the next lesson. This will perfect the skill and give them joy as they realize that they can do something they couldn't do before!

4. Make sure that they clean up after themselves. This is just as important to teach as is doing the project.

5. After you have completed the book, check their skills. *If you think they could benefit from doing the curriculum a second time, start over until they are ready to go on to the next level*. Remember, always continue to have them use the skills they have learned.

Happy Homemaking!
A. B. Leaver and Friends

CONTENTS

Week One - Nutrition.. 6
Week Two - Cooking: Learning to Peel........................ 10
Week Three - Cooking: Using the Toaster...................14
Week Four - Cooking: Cooking with Eggs...................18
Week Five - Cooking: Using the Stove........................22
Week Six - Cooking: Learning about Salads................26
Week Seven - Cooking: Cooking your First Hot Meal............30
Week Eight - Cooking: Beginning Garnishing......................34
Week Nine - Baking: Introducing the Oven...................38
Week Ten - Baking: Following Directions....................42
Week Eleven - Baking: Beginning Coating.....................46
Week Twelve - Baking: Using the Pastry Cutter...................50
Week Thirteen - Baking: Using the Rolling Pin................54
Week Fourteen - Baking: Intro to Sifting....................58
Week Fifteen - Baking: Baking and Cooking a Meal..............62
Week Sixteen - Baking: Learning to Use a Grater...............66
Week Seventeen - Cleaning: Using a Vacuum......................70
Week Eighteen - Cleaning: Learning to Dust...................74
Week Nineteen - Cleaning: How to Sweep Properly..............78
Week Twenty - Cleaning: How to Wash the Dishes...............82
Week Twenty-One - Cleaning: How to Make a Bed...............86
Week Twenty-Two - Sewing: Learning to Stitch....................90
Week Twenty-Three - Sewing: Backwards & Forwards............94
Week Twenty-Four - Sewing: Cutting a Pattern...................98
Week Twenty-Five - Sewing: Sewing on Applique (Patterns)....102
Week Twenty-Six - Organizing: What is Organization?............106
Week Twenty-Seven - Organization: How to Organize a Close.110
Week Twenty-Eight - Organization: Organizing the Bookshelf.114
Week Twenty-Nine - Hospitality: It's Time for Company!..........118
Week Thirty - Reviewing Level One................................122

"He causeth the grass to grow for the cattle, and herb for the service of man: that he may bring forth food out of the earth..."

Psalm 104:14

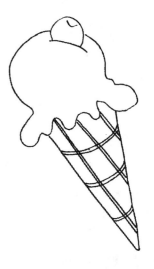

Nutrition

Week One
NUTRITION

This is Faith. Faith is going to teach you a bit about nutrition.

She is sitting down eating her favorite foods, but her mother is telling her that she should only eat a little bit. Why?

Have you ever eaten too much? What happens to your tummy?

Have you ever gotten sick from eating too much candy? What happens to your body?

Remember that your body is God's temple. We must take very good care of it.

Faith has a puppy. His name is Lad. What would happen to Lad if Faith only fed him candy? Would he be healthy? Just as puppies need to eat nutritious puppy food, so should we eat healthy food, too!

The following food groups are necessary for our bodies to grow:

Nutrition

1. Breads
2. Dairy
3. Proteins
4. Fruits
5. Vegetables
6. Junk food

TASK: This week, choose one meal each day; write down and list which foods belong to which group. Make sure that you also list how much junk food you eat.

At the end of the week show your list to your mother and have her check your work. She will help you figure out if all your foods are listed in the correct group.

This task will help prepare you to feed your own family with healthy, balanced meals when you grow up!

"It is God who giveth food to all flesh; for His mercy endureth forever."

Psalm 136:25

Cooking

Week Two

Peeling Properly

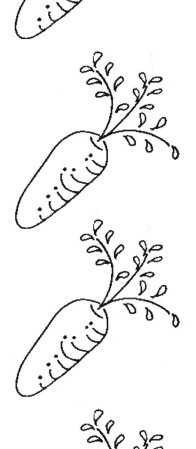

Faith is learning how to prepare food for cooking. What is she doing to the carrots?

Have you ever peeled carrots? Potatoes? This can be done safely and efficiently, if you know how to do it properly.

What is this cooking utensil below?

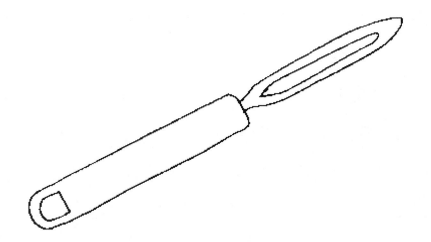

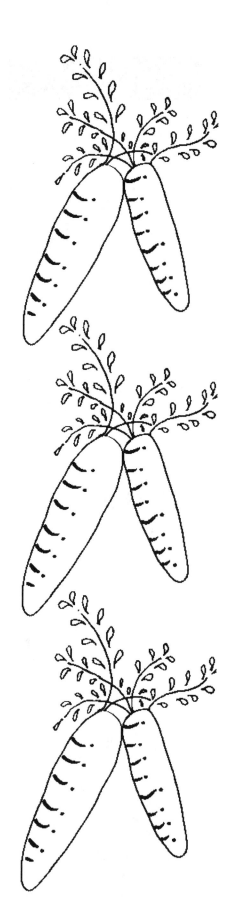

Why do we peel our food for preparation?

1. If you purchase your food from stores, there have been many hands that have touched the food. Peeling makes sure that it is sanitized.

2. Many of our food preparers spray chemicals on our food. Washing doesn't remove it all. Peeling makes sure that it is completely eliminated from our food.

3. Appearance - How our food looks is also important. It is our duty as cooks to make our food appear as pretty and tasteful as possible. Peeling also rids our carrots and potatoes from black spots, imbedded dirt and unseen micro-organisms.

If you grow your own food, you may not have to peel, as there are not as many dangerous pesticides on the food. Just scrub it clean and cook.

A Carrot Tray

1. Count how many people you are going to feed. Allow one carrot for each person.

2. Wash and have mother show you the correct way to peel your carrots. (Always peel away from you.)

3. Carefully, cut off both ends. Cut your carrot in half.

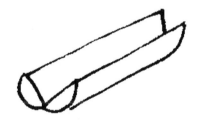

4. Next, use this garnish tool to cut your carrot in half, length-wise, and then half again.

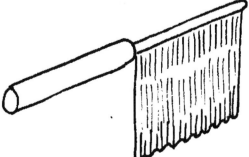

5. Place on tray and serve.

1. Practice making your carrot tray three times this week.

2. Also practice helping mother peel potatoes.

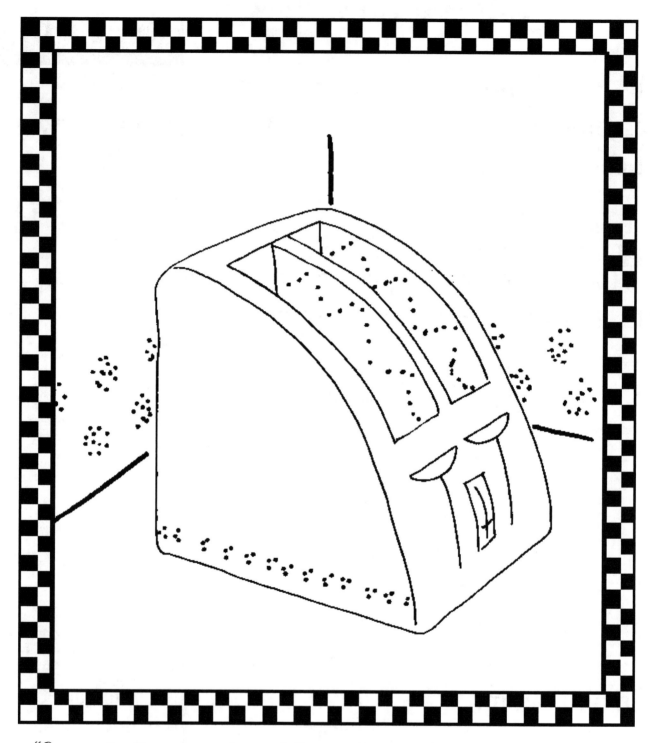

"Remove far from me vanity and lies: give me neither poverty nor riches; feed me with food convenient for me."

Proverbs 30:8

The Toaster

Faith is using the toaster and has always been very careful. She has never been burned because she listened to her mother and followed the rules below:

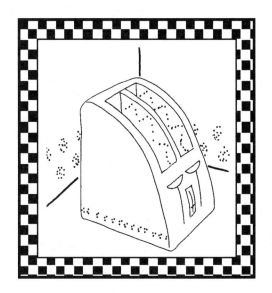

1. Always wash and *dry* your hands before using the toaster. (You don't want to get shocked because your hands are wet.)

2. Have mother check to see if the toaster settings are correct. (You don't want your toast to burn.)

3. Wait until the toaster pops up on its own. Don't force it up because you may get burnt.

Faith's Cinnamon Toast

Safety tip:
Never touch a hot cooking surface, including the toaster, as it is cooking.

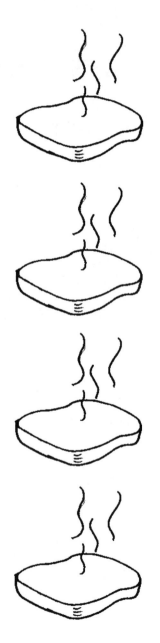

Equipment:
Toaster
Butter Knife
Measuring spoons
Shaker (you can use a salt shaker)

Ingredients:
2 slices of bread
Softened butter or margarine
1/4 cup of sugar
1 tablespoon ground cinnamon

1. Did you complete rules (1) one and (2) two from page 16? If you did, then you are ready to place your bread in the toaster.

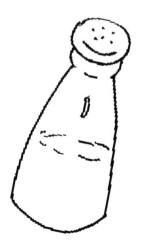

Cooking

2. Wait until the toast pops up and then count to twenty. You don't want to burn your fingers when touching the toast. Be very careful not to touch the toaster itself as it is very hot for about five minutes after it toasts.

3. Spread the toast right away with the softened butter. It melts and tastes the best that way!

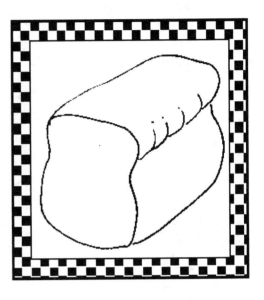

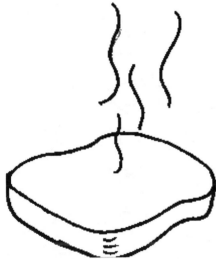

4. You need to make your cinnamon and sugar mixture. Simply place the cinnamon and sugar in your shaker, covering holes with your hand. Place the lid back on and shake until both ingredients are combined. Now shake over the top of your buttered toast!

"And my hand hath found as a nest the riches of the people; and as one gathereth eggs that are left, have I gathered all the earth."

Isaiah 10:13-15

Cooking

Week Four

Cooking With Eggs

Have you ever eaten an egg shell in your food? It is something you will never forget once you have done it! It is gritty, sandy, and coarse, all at the same time!

Faith has mastered the art of cracking eggs and you can do it too!

Can you think of some things that you eat that contain eggs?

Many baked and cooked goods contain eggs, even though you can't see them. For example, cakes, cookies, casseroles, souffles (pronounced soo - flays), and more.

```
┌─────────────────────────┐
│     CHECK LIST:         │
│                         │
│ 1.  Apron on?           │
│ 2.  Hair pulled         │
│ back?                   │
│ 3.  Hands washed?       │
│ 4.  Read recipe?        │
│ 5.  Hot pads and        │
│ mitts?                  │
└─────────────────────────┘
```

Cracking eggs:

There are two ways to do it:

1. Cracking on the side of a bowl. You tap the egg on the edge of a dish.

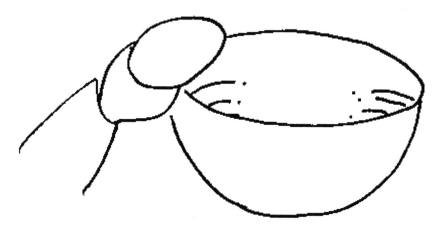

2. Cracking with a knife. You tap the knife on the side of the egg.

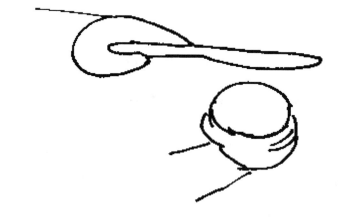

Practice cracking your eggs a few times and then make the following scrambled egg recipe with your mother's help.

Scrambled Eggs

Cooking

Equipment:

Electric fry pan   Trash for shells
Spatula   Bowl
Fork

Ingredients:

1 egg per person   Salt
Butter   Pepper

1. Have mother turn the skillet on for you. Place a small pat of butter (about the thickness of your thumb) in the pan.
2. Beat your eggs in the bowl with a fork.
3. After butter melts, place your eggs in the skillet.
4. Cook the eggs as you stir.
5. Turn eggs onto a plate and serve.

　　See, you can now cook eggs!

"And he will take your daughters to be confectionaries, and to be cooks, and to be bakers."

I Samuel 8:12-14

Cooking

Using the Stove

Faith and her mother are learning to cook on top of the stove. Here are a few rules to follow in order to safely and efficiently use the stove top:

1. Place your pan on the stove and only turn it on when you are there to watch it.

2. Keep a hand on the pan's handle when you are stirring.

3. Always watch your heat. Have mother help you to turn the heat down if your food starts to burn.

4. Be cautious. This is the most important rule of all.

Your Mitt

Don't forget that you have a mitt to use! When holding on to a hot pan or pot when you need to stir, it is invaluable. Try using the smaller version of the mitts or pot holders rather than the large ones. They are easier to use and also less likely to accidentally get near a hot burner.

Frenchy Toast

CHECK LIST:

1. Apron on?
2. Hair pulled back?
3. Hands washed?
4. Read recipe?
5. Hot pads and mitts?

Equipment:

Small bowl	Hand egg beater
Mixing spoon	Measuring cup
Shallow pan	Skillet
Spatula	
Measuring spoons	

Ingredients:

2 eggs	1/2 cup milk
1/4 tsp. salt	4-5 slices bread
3 tbsp. butter	Powdered sugar
Syrup	

1. Now that you can crack eggs, crack 2 eggs into a bowl.

2. With the beater, (have mother help you with this tool) beat the eggs until they are fluffy and then stir in the milk and salt and beat some more.

3. Pour the egg mixture into the shallow pan.

Cooking

4. Dip the bread into the egg mixture, coating each side thoroughly.

5. Heat butter in skillet and then place your bread with egg in the skillet to cook. Cook until toasty brown.

6. When finished, place on your plate and sprinkle with powdered sugar.

7. Serve with maple syrup.

Practice making this for your whole family, counting two pieces

"Every moving thing that liveth shall be meat for you; even as the green
herb have I given you all things."

Genesis 9:2-4

Cooking

Week Six

Learning About Salads

Faith has learned that salads are an important food item to keep her strong and healthy.

When making a salad, remember the following:

1. Romaine and dark green/red leafy lettuces are very good for you. Try to stay away from iceberg lettuce as it has very little nutritional value.

2. Peel your carrots and cucumbers before you slice them for your salad. Keep pieces small, and bite size.

3. Never cut your lettuce with a knife as this causes it to become brown and bruised. Tear your lettuce in small pieces.

4. Wash your vegetables thoroughly.

CHECK LIST:

1. Apron on?
2. Hair pulled back?
3. Hands washed?
4. Read recipe?
5. Hot pads and mitts?

Leafy Garden Salad

Equipment:
Large salad bowl
Salad spoon and fork
Knife
Cutting board
Measuring cup

Ingredients:
1/2 head lettuce
2 stalks celery, sliced (1/2 cup)
4 radishes, sliced (1/2 cup)
2 peeled carrots, sliced (1/2 cup)
1/4 cup of your favorite salad dressing

1. Wash vegetables. Peel carrots.

2. Tear lettuce into bite size pieces.

3. Slice all your vegetables very carefully with a knife. Have mother show you the correct way to press down on the vegetables in order to cut.

4. Place all the vegetables together in bowl.

5. With salad spoon and fork, mix your salad carefully.

Cooking

6. Pour the salad dressing over the top of your salad and mix (toss) carefully.

TASK: Practice making this salad all week long. You can add different ingredients such as cucumbers, onions, cheese, turkey luncheon meat, almonds, and bread cubes (croutons).

"...Make me savoury meat, that I may eat, and bless thee before the Lord before my death."

Genesis 27:7

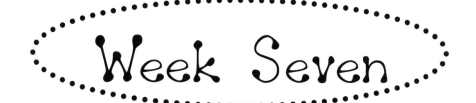

Cooking

Week Seven

Cooking Your First Hot Meal

Faith has done something great! She has finally completed cooking her first meal for her family. Her older sister, Hope, was quite impressed.

Here are some rules to remember:

1. Wear an apron to keep your clothes clean.

2. Have your hair pulled back, so it will not get in your food.

3. Wash hands thoroughly.

4. Read the recipe through once to see if you have all the ingredients.

5. Have hot pads and mitts close by.

Faith's Bottomless Stew

Equipment:
Large soup pot
Cooking spoon
Cutting board
Knife
Peeler
Mitt

Ingredients:
8 cups water
8 beef bouillon cubes
4 carrots, peeled and sliced
1 small onion, peeled, sliced
4 stalks celery, cleaned and sliced
1/2 pound roast beef deli meat, cut   into 1/2 inch pieces
3 peeled potatoes, cut into 1/2 inch   pieces

1. Place your water in the pot on top of the stove. Add the bouillon cubes. Turn burner to medium-high.

Cooking

2. Wash all your vegetables.

3. Peel and slice vegetables.

4. Add prepared vegetables to the pot.

5. Turn on high and bring to a boil, then turn down heat and simmer with a lid on for 30 minutes.

6. After 30 minutes of simmering vegetables, add chopped meat. Now simmer for 30 minutes more.

7. Serve in bowls with bread. This is a fully balanced meal and you can serve it for lunch or dinner!

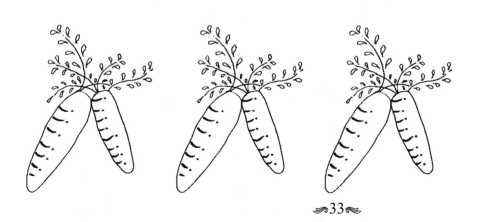

"And she gave the savoury meat and the bread, which she had prepared, into the hand of her son Jacob."

Genesis 27:17

Cooking

Week Eight

Beginning Garnishing

Do you see Faith's creation on the opposite page? She has made her food into a beautiful object. You can do this with many types of vegetables and other foods. It makes the food appear tasty and more appealing to the eye. This is called garnishing.

Faith has learned that it is much more fun to garnish her food when serving it, rather than to just place it on the table without prettying it up. Once she started, it was hard to stop!

A Cucumber Flower

CHECK LIST:

1. Apron on?
2. Hair pulled back?
3. Hands washed?
4. Read recipe?
5. Hot pads and mitts?

Equipment:
1 Sharp knife
1 mixing bowl
Toothpicks
Cutting board

Ingredients:
1 Cucumber
1 Tbsp. salt
Water

1. Slice the cucumber into very thin slices. (So they are transparent.) Soak slices in 1 quart of water with 1 tbsp. of salt for six minutes.

2. Take the smallest slice and roll it up tightly.

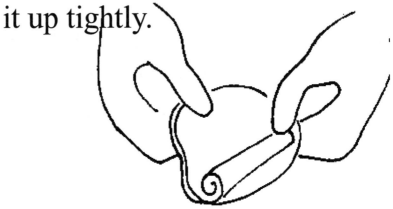

3. Take the next smallest piece and wrap it around the first. Secure with toothpicks

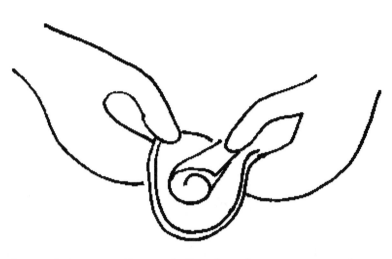

4. Wrap the third piece on the opposite side of the last one. Do this about eight more times. Voila!

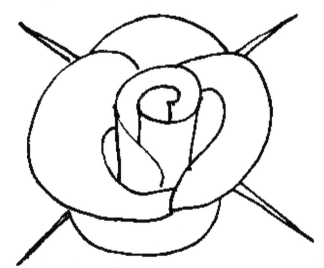

TASK: This week, check a garnishing book out from your local library and practice a few more artistic food designs.

"Man did eat angels' food; He sent them meat to the full."

Psalm 78:25

Baking

Week Nine

Introducing the Oven

I'm sure that you have seen your mother use her oven ever since you were little. With her help, you, too, are going to be learning to use this wonderful tool.

When you use the oven it is called *"baking"*.

Faith has baked up a delicious recipe. She has made a simple cake that is so much fun to make!

This week we are going to learn about ingredients and how to measure them when we bake.

Shaker Cake

CHECK LIST:

1. Apron on?
2. Hair pulled back?
3. Hands washed?
4. Read recipe?
5. Hot pads and mitts?

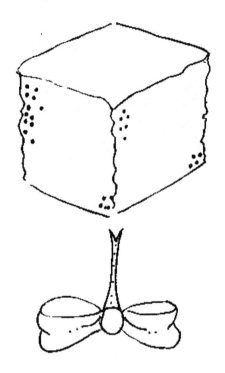

Equipment:
1 Oblong cake pan
Measuring cups and spoons
Mixing bowl
Small bowl for cracking eggs
Wooden spoon
2 Quart jar with lid (If you do not have this, you can even use a plastic drink pitcher if it has a lid that seals tightly.)

Ingredients:
2 cups flour
3 teaspoon baking powder
1 teaspoon salt
4 eggs
1 cup sugar
1 cup oil
1 cup orange juice
Powdered sugar

1. Have mother help you preheat the oven to 375 degrees. Grease your oblong cake pan.

2. With mother's help, measure your dry ingredients in your bowl and set aside.

3. Crack your eggs in a small bowl.

4. Pour eggs into your jar with lid and shake about 20 times.

5. Add the sugar, oil and orange juice and shake until all is blended.

6. Add the dry ingredients and shake again until everything is very smooth and blended.

7. Pour your batter into the greased pan. Bake for 30-35 minutes or until mother can touch the top of the cake and it doesn't go in.

8. Let the cake cool.

9. Sprinkle powdered sugar over the top with a spoon.

10. Serve and enjoy!

TASK: Practice making this again during the week.

Baking

"Obey them that have the rule over you, and submit yourselves; for they watch for your souls, as they that must give account, that they may do it with joy, and not with grief; for that is unprofitable for you."

Hebrews 13:16-18

Baking

Following Directions

One important rule to follow was the one telling us to read the recipe.

Since you are beginning to become a real chef, you will find that the recipes become a bit longer as time goes on. This means that you are simply getting great at baking!

Don't forget... It is important that you always read through your recipes before you start baking. Make sure that you have all the ingredients before you start your baking project.

Beginner's Pizza

<u>CHECK LIST:</u>

1. Apron on?
2. Hair pulled back?
3. Hands washed?
4. Read recipe?
5. Hot pads and mitts?

<u>Equipment:</u>
Wooden spoon
Knife
Cookie sheet

<u>Ingredients:</u>
1 - 15 oz. can tomato sauce
Garlic powder
1 can buttermilk biscuits
Oregano
1 cup shredded mozzarella cheese

1. Preheat the oven to 400 degrees.

2. Open biscuit can and spread each biscuit out like a flat little pizza on your cookie sheet (with clean hands).

3. Open your tomato sauce and evenly spoon out sauce onto each pizza.

4. Shake your garlic powder on

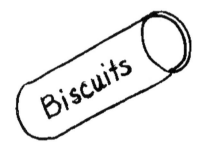

top of each pizza.

6. Take a pinch of oregano between your fingers and sprinkle it over each pizza.

7. Sprinkle your cheese over the top of each little pizza.

8. Have mother help you turn the oven to 400 degrees.

9. Place cookie sheet in the oven with your oven mitts. Bake for 7-10 minutes or until the cheese is melted and the dough is cooked.

"And the Lord thy God will make thee plenteous in every work of thine hand, in the fruit of thy body, and in the fruit of thy cattle, and in the fruit of thy land, for good."

Deuteronomy 30:9

Baking

Week Eleven

Beginning Coating

Do you know what it means to "coat food"? No, this isn't when you put little coats on your chicken breasts!

When you "coat your food" you are learning to really "dip and roll". Can you think of some foods that you have eaten that are coated? Well, fried chicken has an egg and flour coating. Some meatballs are dipped in egg and rolled in flour. Surprisingly, so are some cookies!

This week *you* are going to learn to coat food!

Easy Oven-Fried Chicken

CHECK LIST:

1. Apron on?
2. Hair pulled back?
3. Hands washed?
4. Read recipe?
5. Hot pads and mitts?

Equipment:
Large lasagna pan
Large flat dish to roll in
Fork

Ingredients:
2 pounds of skinned, cut up chicken (thawed frozen chicken tenderloins work great)
1 1/2 cups bread crumbs
1 teaspoon salt
1 teaspoon pepper
1/2 teaspoon garlic salt
1/2 teaspoon onion powder
1 cup mayonnaise

Have mother preheat oven to 375 degrees.

1. In a casserole dish, mix your bread crumbs, salt and pepper, garlic

salt and onion powder well.

2. Take each piece of chicken and with clean hands, spread mayonaisse on surface.

3. Next, place it in your bread crumb mixture and roll until it is thickly coated. Place in your large lasagna pan. Repeat this procedure until all of your chicken is completely coated.

4. Place in the oven and bake uncovered for 30-35 minutes.

5. Have mother remove it from the oven and serve with a salad which you can now make on your own!

TASK: Practice making this once again during the week.

Baking

"For God shall bring every work into judgment, with every secret thing, whether it be good, or whether it be evil."

Ecclesiastes 12:13-15

Using the Pastry Cutter

Do you know what instrument Faith is using? It is called a pastry cutter.

What is "pastry"?

Below are some examples of pastries. Can you name them?

Cinnamon Crusties

CHECK LIST:

1. Apron on?
2. Hair pulled back?
3. Hands washed?
4. Read recipe?
5. Hot pads and mitts?

Equipment:
Cookie sheet
Mixing bowl
Pastry cutter
Knife

Ingredients:
2 cups flour
1 1/2 teaspoons salt
1/2 cup salad oil
5 tablespoons cold water
Mix together:
1/2 cup sugar
1/2 teaspoon cinnamon

Preheat oven to 375 degrees.

1. Combine your salt and flour in a mixing bowl.

2. Pour the oil and cold water into

a measuring cup but do not mix together. Quickly pour the oil and cold water into the salt and flour mixture.

Baking

3. With your pastry cutter, cut the mixture until it resembles crumbs.

4. With clean hands, form the pastry into two balls.

5. On a clean surface, sprinkle some flour to stop sticking, and place one ball on top. Flatten with your fists and spread out like you would pizza.

6. Sprinkle your flattened dough with sugar and cinnamon mixture to your liking.

7. Cut in strips and place on cookie sheet. Bake for 10-15 minutes until golden. Serve.

"Let your light so shine before men, that they may see your good works, and glorify your Father which is in heaven."

Matthew 5:16

Baking

Week Thirteen

Using the Rolling Pin

Do you see what Faith has? It is called a rolling pin. Do you know what you use the rolling pin for?

In last week's lesson you learned how to make pastry. Do you remember how you spread out the dough with your hands? Did you know that there is an easier way to do this? It is much easier to use a rolling pin. It is a baker's helper, and it cuts down on time and work.

Let's learn how to use the rolling pin in this week's project!

Bisquick Biscuits

CHECK LIST:

1. Apron on?
2. Hair pulled back?
3. Hands washed?
4. Read recipe?
5. Hot pads and mitts?

Equipment:
Cookie sheet
Rolling pin
Mixing bowl
Measuring cups
Round cutter or medium size glass

Ingredients:
2 1/4 cups Bisquick
3/4 cup milk

Preheat oven to 450 degrees.

1. Stir the ingredients until they form a soft dough.

2. With clean hands, knead the dough on a clean, lightly floured counter top for about two minutes.

3. Make sure that there is a thin layer of flour on the counter top and

then sprinkle a bit on top of your dough. Take your rolling pin and coat it with flour.

Baking

4. Roll your dough from the middle out. Go from north, south, east and west. When your dough is 1/2 of an inch thick, stop.

5. Take a round cookie cutter or a medium glass. Dip in flour so it won't stick and then make round biscuits. Place finished dough biscuits on your cookie sheet.

6. Take remaining dough and roll again and repeat process until all the dough is used.

7. Bake at 450 degrees for 7-9 minutes. Serve with jam or honey.

TASK: Practice making this once or twice again this week.

"Now there was at Joppa a certain disciple named Tabitha, which by in-
terpretation is called Dorcas. This woman was full of good works and
almsdeeds which she did."

Acts 9:36

Week Fourteen

Beginning Sifting

Faith is sifting flour. This week, you are going to learn a little about sifting with your mother's help.

First, you need to find a kitchen sifter. It looks like this:

CHECK LIST:

1. Apron on?
2. Hair pulled back?
3. Hands washed?
4. Read recipe?
5. Hot pads and mitts?

Faith's Chocolate Chip Bars

Equipment:
Sifter
Oblong cake pan
Mixing bowl
Wooden spoon
Spatula
Measuring cups and spoons
Knife
Cutting Board

Ingredients:
1/4 pound butter
1 pound brown sugar
3 eggs
2 cups sifted flour
1/2 teaspoon salt
1 teaspoon baking powder
1 teaspoon vanilla extract
1/2 cup chopped walnuts
1 6-oz. package semisweet chocolate chips
(Preheat oven to 350 degrees)

1. Cream butter and brown sugar together. Add eggs and beat some more.

2. Sift the flour with the salt and baking powder. Have mother help you the very first time.

3. Stir in the flour, salt, baking powder, vanilla, walnuts and chocolate chips. Blend well.

4. Pour into a greased, oblong cake pan. Bake for 20-25 minutes.

5. Cool and cut into bars.

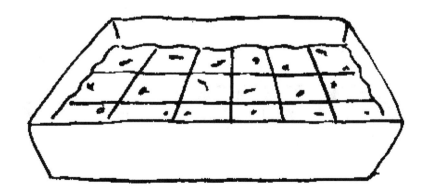

TASK: Practice making this one or two times more this week.

"But glory, honour, and peace, to every man that worketh good..."

Romans 2:10

Baking

Week Fifteen

Baking and Cooking a Meal

Did you know that sometimes you will find that you need to both cook and bake when making a recipe? This happens many times when working with meat or when you make a casserole dish ahead of time.

Usually, you first have to cook the meat and other ingredients on top of the stove.

Next, you place it together as the recipe tells you to, and then you bake it in the oven.

Faith has made a "Beef Pie". This week you are going to make it too!

Faith's Beef Pie

CHECK LIST:

1. Apron on?
2. Hair pulled back?
3. Hands washed?
4. Read recipe?
5. Hot pads and mitts?

Equipment:
Skillet
Spatula
Mixing bowl
Spoon
Measuring cups
Oblong casserole dish

Ingredients:
2 1/2 cups frozen mixed vegetables
1 pound ground beef
2 cans cream of mushroom soup
2 cups Bisquick
1 cup milk
2 eggs
Pam
(Preheat oven to 400 degrees)

1. With mother's help, brown ground beef in a skillet. Have her drain off the fat, and watch how she does it so you can do it too.

2. Add vegetables and soup to skillet and mix completely with heat off.

3. In mixing bowl, combine Bisquick, milk and eggs.

4. Spray the bottom of your casserole dish with Pam, and then spread your meat mixture evenly over the bottom.

5. Next, with a spoon, drop the Bisquick mixture over the meat and then spread so that it is evenly distributed.

6. Bake for 30-35 minutes or until the top is golden brown.

Baking

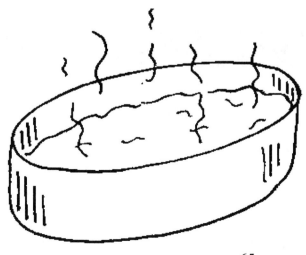

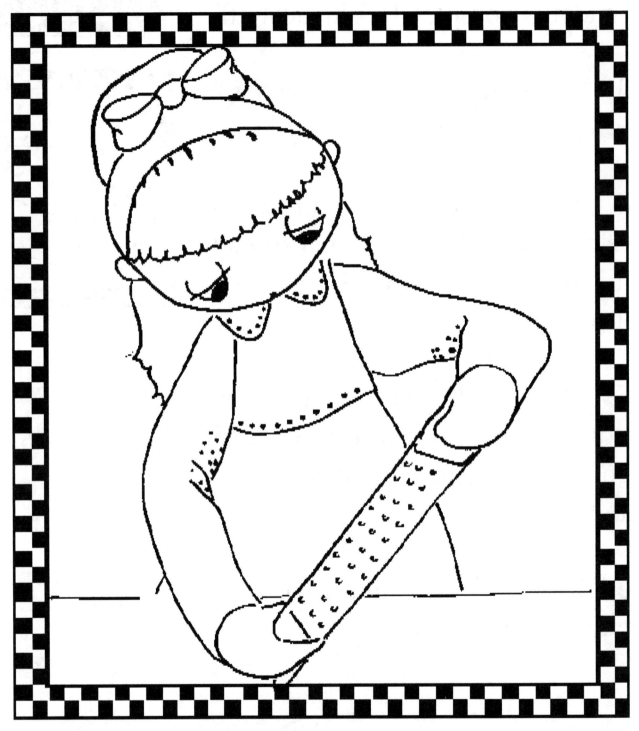

"And God is able to make all grace abound toward you; that ye, always having all sufficiency in all things, may abound to every good work."

2 Corinthians 9:8

Baking

Week Sixteen

Learning to Use a Grater

Do you see what Faith is using? It is a grater.

Have you ever had a taco from a fast food drive-thru? What is the cheese like? It is grated. This week you are going to learn to use a grater, too!

Faith is making one of her most favorite dishes of all time. She loves eating Mexican food and her big sister, Hope, has taught her how to make a Mexican pie.

It has almost everything in it from each food group with the exception of fruit. Let's try her recipe!

Mexican Pie

CHECK LIST:

1. Apron on?
2. Hair pulled back?
3. Hands washed?
4. Read recipe?
5. Hot pads and mitts?

Equipment:
Skillet
Wooden spoon
Measuring cups and spoons
Square baking casserole dish
Grater
Beater

Ingredients:
1 small onion
1 tablespoon oil
1 pound ground beef
1 can tomatoes (14 oz)
1 can kernel corn, drained (14 oz)
1 1/2 teaspoon salt & chili powder
1 cup corn meal
1 cup milk
2 beaten eggs
1 cup grated Cheddar cheese
(Preheat oven to 350 degrees)

1. Cook the onion until clear in a

skillet in 1 tablespoon of oil.

2. Add the meat and brown. Have mother help you pour off fat.

3. Add the vegetables and seasonings and bring to a boil.

4. Pour mixture into a square casserole dish.

5. In a mixing bowl, combine the cornmeal, milk and eggs. Pour over the meat mixture.

6. Now it is time to grate your cheese. Have mother observe you as you learn to do this. Sprinkle the cheese over the corn meal mixture. Bake one hour. Let stand for ten minutes then serve.

TASK: Practice making this one more time this week.

Baking

"And God is able to make all grace abound toward you; that ye, always
having all sufficiency in all things, may abound to every good work."

2 Corinthians 9:8

Cleaning

Week Seventeen

Using a Vacuum

We are on to a new section of learning! We are going to learn about cleaning our home.

One of the most important tools that God has given us is a vacuum. Why is it important? Dust mites live in dust. They are tiny insects which can cause allergies and other unpleasant symptoms. The vacuum helps us to keep our homes free from dust mites and the reactions we have to them.

Have you helped your mother vacuum before? If you have, you probably can whiz right through this lesson!

Using a Vacuum

Remember...

All vacuums are different.

Take a little time to explore your mother's vacuum.

1. Have mother show you her vacuum. Many vacuums differ so you will need her help when using this material. Where is the on/off switch?

2. What are each of these attachments used for?

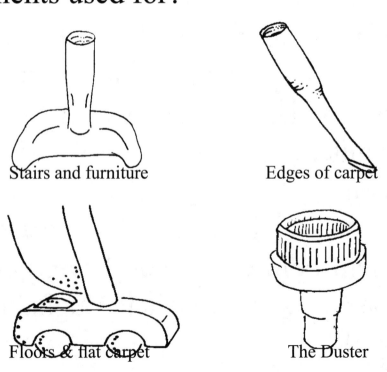

Stairs and furniture

Edges of carpet

Floors & flat carpet

The Duster

3. *Changing the bag.* Inside the vacuum there is a bag which collects all the dirt and dust that it sucks up. This needs to be changed whenever it is full. Symptoms that show that a bag is full: a) Suction will diminish or disappear completely. b) You will notice that little crumbs on the floor are still there after you have vacuumed. c) The air where you are vacuuming will start to get very dusty. Have mother show you how to change the bag in her vacuum.

Cleaning

TASK: This week plan on vacuuming the following with mother showing you the correct way:

1. A floor with carpet.
2. Some stairs.
3. A non-carpeted floor.
4. The edge of a carpeted room.
5. Using the duster for a bookshelf.

"Comfort your hearts, and establish you in every good word and work."

2 Thessalonians 2:17

Cleaning

Week Eighteen
Learning to Dust

When you are cleaning your home, it is always good to remember to always vacuum first and then dust. If you dust first, your vacuum will undo all the hard work you have completed. It will spread a thin layer of dust over everything! This is because it has an exhaust system that lets out a little bit of dust.

Have you ever helped mother to dust? There are different ways to dust different objects in your house. You wouldn't use oil on glass, nor would you use ammonia on wood. It would ruin your mother's furniture. Let's learn the correct way to dust!

What you need when dusting:

-Two cloths, old towels or diapers work great!

-Vinegar and water solution (1/2 to 1/2) or window cleaner

-Furniture oil

-Feather duster

When dusting wood furniture:

1. Always remember to use only furniture polish or wood oil for wood furniture. Wood needs moisture and care. You wouldn't use vinegar or window cleaner on wood as it would dry it out and cause the finish to come off.

2. Take the knickknacks off the furniture before you dust, and then clean all the dust off with your cloth. Go over it again to give it a good shine.

Dusting knickknacks:

Cleaning

1. Use your feather duster to dust the tops of books on shelves and knickknacks with lots of edges and grooves.

2. To wash your feather duster, you use an oil based soap, such as Murphy's Oil Soap. Fill up your sink and add 1/4 cup to the warm water. Place your feather duster in the suds and rotate until clean. Hang to dry.

Dusting glass or plastic:

1. Use your cloth and the vinegar and water solution, or window cleaning solution. Go in the same stroking direction.

TASK: This week dust one room completely. Have mother check your work.

"But (which becometh women professing godliness) with good works."

I Timothy 2:10

Cleaning

Week Nineteen

How to Sweep Properly

What is Faith doing? She is sweeping her floor. Why would she want to do this?

We sweep our floors so that our homes will be clean and our bodies healthy.

Imagine what would happen if you never swept your floor. Think about your kitchen. What do you think it might have on it if you never swept? Would bugs like that floor? Do you like bugs?

Let's learn how to sweep!

The four steps of sweeping:

1. In the room you are sweeping, always go around the edges first and bring the debris to the middle of the room.

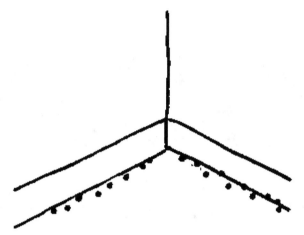

2. Next, sweep from one edge and bring the dirt to the middle pile. Continue around the floor until everything has been swept.

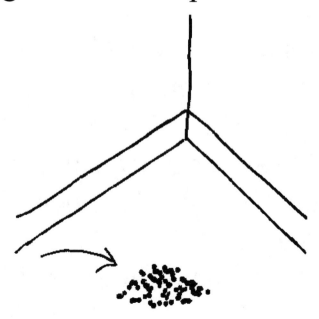

3. Get your dust pan and as you bend over, sweep the dirt into the dust pan.

Cleaning

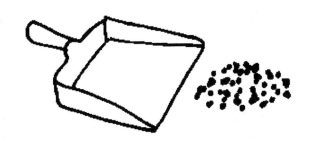

4. Empty everything into the garbage and put the broom back in place.

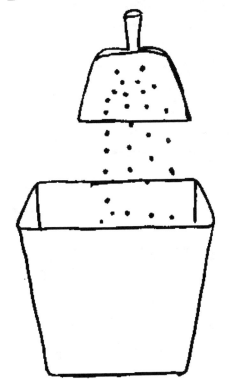

TASK: This week, sweep the kitchen floor every night.

"...Well reported of for good works; if she have brought up children, if she have lodged strangers, if she have washed the saints' feet, if she have relieved the afflicted, if she have diligently followed every good work."

I Timothy 5:9-11

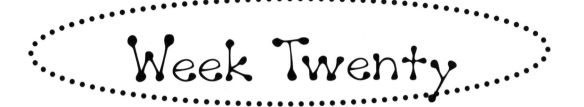

How to Wash the Dishes

Washing dishes has to be one of the most nicest part of dinner time. Faith loves to wash dishes with her older sister, Hope.

They have been washing dishes together ever since she can remember and have it down to a system.

Have you ever washed dishes?

Do you have a dishwasher? Even if you have a dishwasher, you still must wash some items, such as pots and pans. Let's learn how to get those items really, really *clean*!

The four steps of washing dishes:

1. **The Soap Cycle**: Use very warm water, gloves and soap for your dish water.

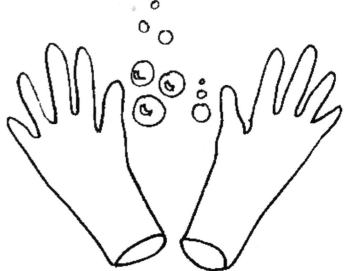

2. **Cleaning**: Wash your pots with a cloth or sponge. Make sure that you get all edges and that you scrub every inch of the dish/pan. If not, you could leave food stuck on, which collects bacteria.

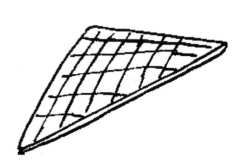

3. **Rinsing**: When rinsing the clean dish/pan, always use hot water. There are two ways of rinsing: 1) Rinsing in the other sink full of hot water, or 2) Rinsing under hot running water. Both work. Ask mother which is better for your home.

4. **Drying**: There are two ways of drying, 1) air drying, or 2) drying with a towel. Air drying you simply place them on the dish rack and let dry by themselves. Or, you can dry with a towel immediately and then put the dishes up where they go.

TASK: This week practice washing all the dishes after dinner. Ask mother for her supervision the very first time, and then you'll be able to tackle it fine on your own!

Cleaning

Anti-bacterial soap is the best choice of soaps as it kills and disinfects the dishes as you clean them. This stops the spreading of nasty germs that cause colds and the flu.

"..(women)... That they do good, that they be rich in good works, ready to distribute, willing to communicate..."

I Timothy 6:18

Cleaning

Week Twenty-One

How to Make a Bed

Faith does something that you do ever single day. Can you guess what that is? She sleeps! All people sleep, and in our country, most people sleep in a bed.

Since this is something that we do every day of our lives, it is very important that we learn to make our beds.

Can you imagine what a bedroom would look like if a person never, ever made their beds?

Faith is going to show you the easy way she makes her bed.

The five easy steps of making a bed: (Have mother help the first time.)

1. Bottom sheet: Stretch over the bed. Top sheet & blanket: Pull the sheet up so that it is level with the top of the bed. Next pull the blanket up so that it is almost to the top.

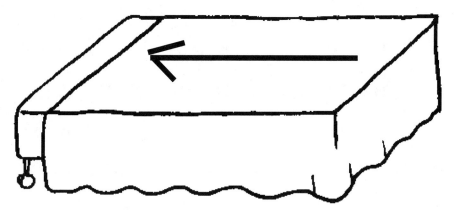

2. Pull your sheets and blankets so that they have equal amounts on the left and right. Pull tight & smooth.

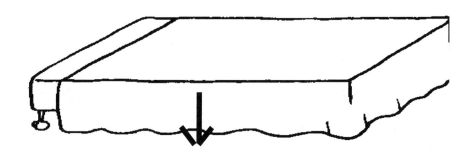

3. Tuck the ends in tight at the foot of the bed. Now fold over the sheet and blanket at the top.

Cleaning

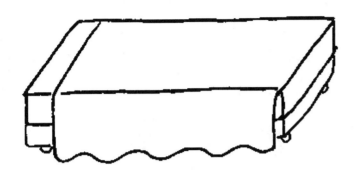

4. Put your arm in to make a triangle on each bottom side and then tuck in the sides tightly.

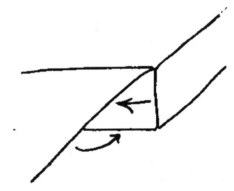

5. Fluff your pillow and lay it on top of the bed. You are done!!!

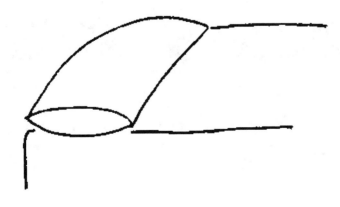

"....That the man of God may be perfect, thoroughly furnished unto all good works."

2 Timothy 3:17

Learning to Stitch

Faith has learned a new skill. She is learning how to sew. Can you think of some reasons why it is important that young ladies learn how to sew?

Faith made the following list:

1. In some cases, sewing is less expensive.

2. Sewing is needed to repair clothing.

3. Sewing is necessary when trying to find modest and wholesome clothing.

4. Sewing can be an art and a personal way of adding feminine touches to clothing.

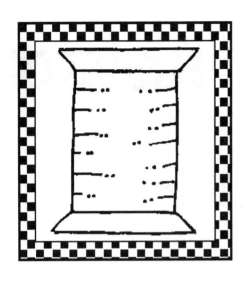

Beginning Stitching:

<u>Equipment:</u>
1 large yarn needle
Yarn
Thick note cards
The following patterns xeroxed
Pencil
Scissors
Hole puncher

1. Have mother xerox the following patterns:

2. Cut these patterns out and trace with a pencil on the thick note cards.

Sewing

3.   With the hole punch, punch holes every 1/2 inch or so around the pattern line.

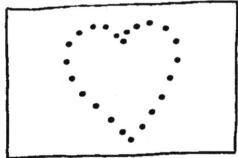

4.   Take your yarn needle and thread it with yarn. Practice sewing in and out on your patterns. When you have mastered this task you are ready for the next project!

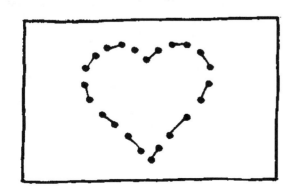

"The Lord will perfect that which concerneth me; thy mercy, O Lord, endureth forever; forsake not the works of thine own hands."

Psalm 138:8

Sewing

Week Twenty-Three

Sewing Backwards & Forwards

Faith has learned to stitch on real fabric! It is so much fun to actually sew on real material and then to examine your stitches.

Do you see the hoop that Faith is using to sew with below? It is called an embroidery hoop and it helps to keep your fabric stable while you sew.

Stitching Backwards & Forwards:

Equipment:
Medium size embroidery hoop
1 large needle
White thread
1 square foot of mother's dark fabric scraps

1.   Have mother watch as you thread your needle. Have her help you make a knot at the end.

2.   With mother's help, place the material in the hoop.

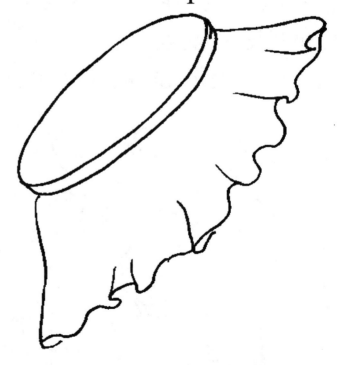

3. Practice sewing in a circle about an inch in from the edge of the hoop. Go from right to left.

4. When you get to the end, turn and in the opposite stitch, sew from left to right. This is what your sewing machine does, but you are doing it by hand.

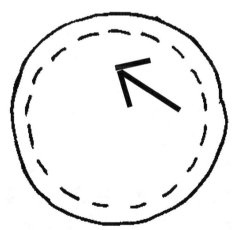

TASK: When you have finished this, do another circle, another inch in. Practice until you can make even, perfect stitches.

"Every wise woman buildeth her house; but the foolish plucketh it down with her hands."

Proverbs 14:1

Week Twenty-Four

Cutting a Pattern

Most sewing projects will have a pattern that you will need to cut.

Have mother enlarge the pattern below so that it is larger than the size of the original:

Making a Beginner's Pincushion

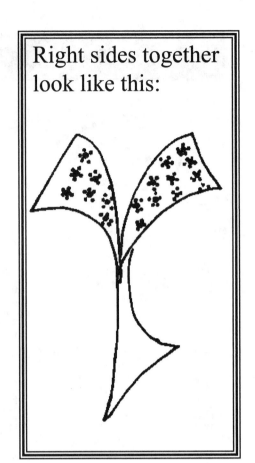

Right sides together look like this:

Equipment:

1/4 yard of fabric (use scraps that mother may have)
   Pattern
   Pins
   Scissors
   Needle
   Thread
   Rice

1. Fold your material in half so that the bright pattern sides (the right sides) are touching. Lay the pattern on top:

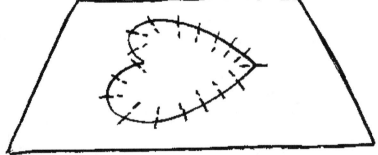

2. Pin the pattern on the fabric as shown above.

3. Cut around the edge of the pattern. Take out pins and remove pattern.

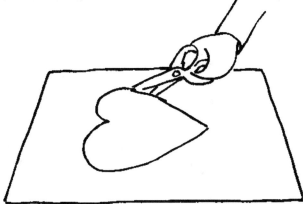

Sewing

4. With right sides still together, sew around the outside edges leaving a 1 inch space for inserting the rice.

stuff rice here

5. Turn inside out and stuff with rice. Sew the hole closed.

"She seeketh wool, and flax, and worketh willingly with her hands."

Proverbs 31:13

Sewing

Week Twenty-Five

Sewing on Applique (Patterns)

Faith has found a wonderful way to personalize her clothing. It is called "applique".

Do you see her pillow on the opposite page? She has appliqued all the designs on it. She actually created them and thought of the patterns all by herself!

This is a fun and easy way to make objects pretty.

Do you know how to sew a "box stitch"? This is what you use for beginning applique.

The "box stitch":

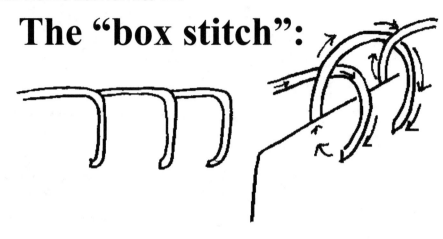

Making a Family Flag

<u>Equipment:</u>
1/2 yard fabric
Mother's fabric scraps
Needle
Thread to match the fabric
Iron (Have mother help you)

1. Iron fabric. Cut your fabric so that it measures 12 inches by 18 inches. Box stitch around the edges.

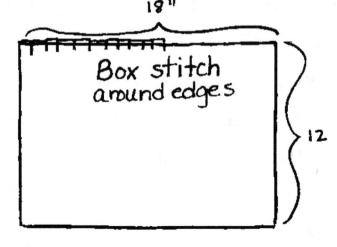

2. Draw on a piece of paper the design you want for your family flag.

Sewing

3. Cut out your pattern, pin the pattern to your colored scrap fabric, and cut out.

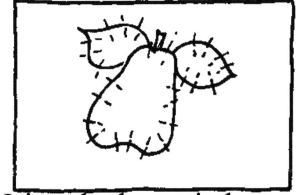

4. Using the box stitch, sew your designs on the flag. Voila!

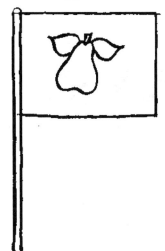

"The desire of the slothful killeth him; for his hands refuse to labour."

Proverbs 21:25

Week Twenty-Six

What is Organization?

Have you ever heard someone say, "I really need to get organized"? What do you think being organized means?

Faith's mother has told her that she needs to get organized. This means that she needs to have a place for everything, and everything in its own place!

Faith has a terrible time with her drawers. She tends to throw everything in all drawers and hasn't been able to find things when she needs them.

Today she is going to learn to organize a drawer!

The four steps to organizing a drawer:

1. Empty everything out of the drawer onto the floor.

2. Toss anything that you haven't used in two years.

3.　Place similar items together. Organize like objects in neat piles in your drawer.

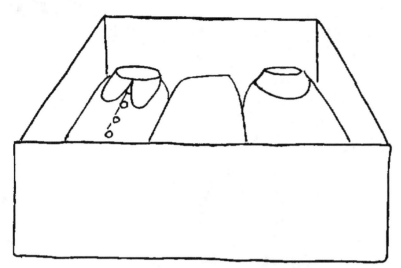

4. Have a certain drawer for each group of belongings you have

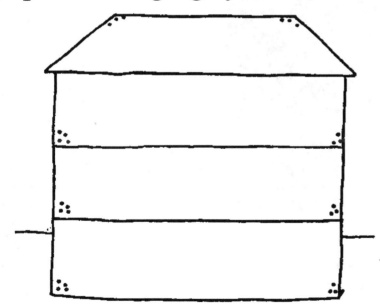

TASK:　This week organize all of your dresser drawers.　How long can you keep them organized before you must sort again?

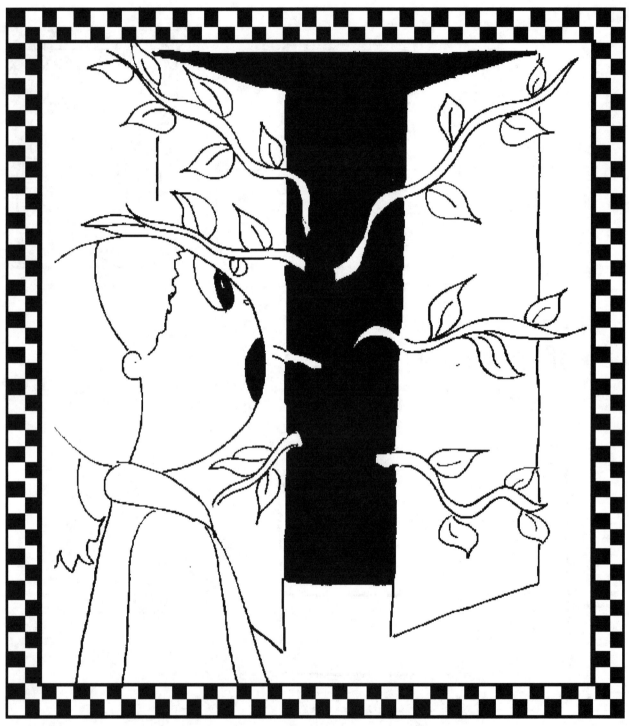

"Better is an handful with quietness, than both the hands full with travail and vexation of spirit."

Ecclesiastes 4:6

Week Twenty-Seven

How to Organize a Closet

Faith has something growing in her closet. It is a clothing pile. Instead of hanging all her clothing in her closet in order, she has tossed them on to the closet floor.

Her mother is going to teach her the easy way of organizing her closet so that she can always find the items she needs.

Do you ever have problems with your closet?

Try the following easy steps and see if you, too, can keep your closet organized...

Five easy steps to organizing a clothes closet:

1. Take out any items on the floor. Organize them in boxes that will fit on one side of the closet. Keep shoes in a hanging organizer.

2. Arrange clothing in like order. For example, hang skirts with skirts, blouses with blouses, and dresses with dresses.

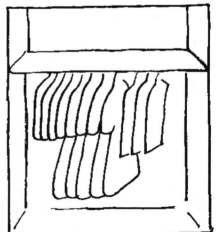

3. Next arrange them in the same color order. Go light to dark.

4. If you have shelves in your closet, place summer clothing, if it is winter, in boxes and stack. Keep them folded nicely in preparation for the changing season.

Organizing

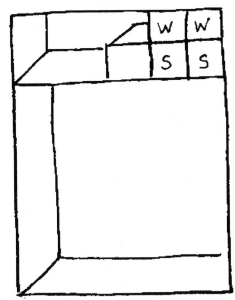

5. Place extra blankets on the other side of the shelf or heavy sweaters.

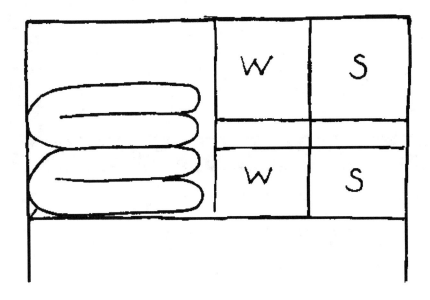

"Let all things be done decently and in order."

1 Corinthians 14:40

Week Twenty-Eight

Organizing a Bookshelf

Faith is homeschooled. In her home, there are many books. Her parents have purchased good books so that they would have a quality library at home, plus she has her school books.

It is very easy to have a million books lying around the house in places where they do not belong. Faith is learning how to organize her bookshelf, and you can learn this simple task too!

Four easy steps to organizing a bookshelf:

1. Remove any knicknacks from your bookshelf. Try to keep all bookshelves for books.

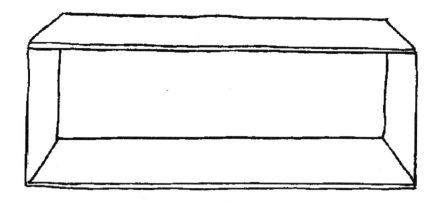

2. Organize your bookshelf in regards to size. Have the top shelf for small paperback books.

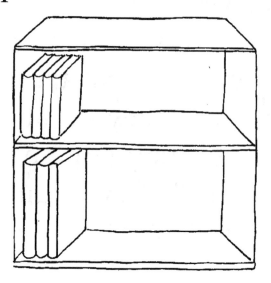

3. On each shelf, again, make sure that you organize according to size. Have the taller books start on the left and place the shorter ones as you go right.

Organization

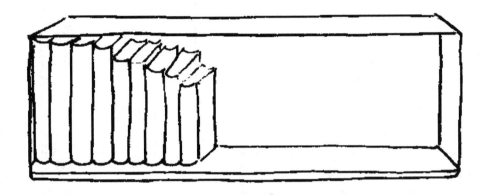

4. If you have loose papers stored on your bookshelf, have these placed in folders and label the outside of the folder with the topic of the papers.

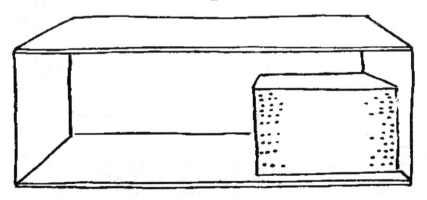

TASK: This week organize your own bookshelves and ask mother if she has any she needs organized.

"Be not forgetful to entertain strangers; for thereby some have entertained angels unawares."

Hebrews 13:2

Week Twenty-Nine

It's Time for Company!

Faith loves to have company. She loves the excitement of preparing for her guests, the happiness of fellowship when friends are visiting, the simple enjoyment of entertaining, and the bittersweet joy of picking up after they are gone.

Her mother has thoughtfully set some guidelines for her as she learns about hospitality and friendship.

These rules might be helpful for you, too, as you have friends over!

The Rules for Hospitality:

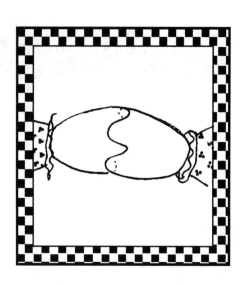

1. When inviting friends over, always offer the invitation with a set time... a beginning and an end.

2. Prepare ahead what you will serve your guests.

3. Prepare an activity for you to do while they are there. (Idle time is wasted time.)

Hospitality

4. Don't whine and complain and ask for more time, when the visiting time is over. Be gracious and kind, and do not make your friend's visit end on a wrong note because you have asked mother for more time and she had to say "no" in front of your guest. This makes them feel bad.

TASK:
With mother's permission, ask a friend over this week, and follow the guidelines given.

"I have fought a good fight, I have finished my course, I have kept the faith."

2 Timothy 4:7

Review

Week Thirty

Reviewing Level One

You have come to the end of the book! Do you feel as if you have learned some things that will help you when you have a home of your own?

Faith's mother gave her a little test to see what she remembered after learning these new things. With your mother's help, you, too, can check to see what you now know.

Simply sit with mother and have her read the questions to you and try to answer them as best you can. There's no problem if you can't remember it all. Even a mom needs to refresh her knowledge sometimes!

1. Why shouldn't you eat too much candy? Name the food groups which you should eat from daily. (Pg.8-9)

2. What tool should you use to peel a carrot? Name three reasons why it is good to peel some of our vegetables. (Pg. 12-13)

3. Describe the correct way to crack an egg. (Pg. 20)

4. Tell the four rules for using the stove top. (Pg. 23)

5. Why shouldn't you cut your lettuce? (Pg. 27)

6. Name the five rules for cooking. (Pg. 30)

7. What is "garnishing"? (Pg. 35)

8. What is the difference between baking and cooking? (Pg. 39)

9. When you coat a piece of chicken, do you roll it in the flour or egg first? (Pg. 49)

10. Do you use scissors when you "cut" pastry? (Pg. 51)

11. Which object do you use with

cheese in order to achieve small pieces for tacos? (Pg. 67)

12. Name the four attachments for a vacuum and describe what each is used for. (Pg. 72)

13. What type of solution would you use for dusting glass? For wood? (Pg. 76-77)

14. What are the four rules of sweeping? (Pg. 80-81)

15. What is the correct order of the following steps when washing dishes? Drying, Cleaning, Rinsing, the Soap Cycle (Pg. 84-85)

16. What were some of Faith's reasons to sew? (Pg. 91)

17. Why should you organize your drawers, closets and bookshelves? In detail, explain how to organize your books. (Pg. 116-117)

18. What is hospitality? What should you do when you would like to have company? (Pg. 120-121)

Hospitality

Special thanks to Anne White, whose help and knowledge has been more than invaluable. Anne became a professional chef after her children were raised. She has spent much of her time teaching younger (and older!) women how to bake and cook, and many other home care skills. Now in her 80's, she has patiently offered her advice and wisdom in order for us to be able to lovingly create this book. We hope you enjoy this material as much as we have enjoyed learning from her and putting it together!

A quick note to mother,

If your child is a young six and still needs help with these projects, before going on to the next level, we recommend starting this book over again.

By doing this, the child becomes more familiar and confident with each project and can whiz through the tasks with ease.

Continue to the next level after they have mastered the skills listed in this book. Each future level contains a quick review of past levels and then offers a more difficult challenge for them to master as they continue on.

Happy homemaking!

A. B. Leaver & Friends

ORDER FORM

___Narrow Way Character Curriculum $32.95
(Includes 8 Pearable Kingdom Stories-Are not repeated in Volumes Below)

Pearables Kingdom Stories:
___ Volume 1 $17.50
___ Volume 2 $17.50
___ Volume 3 $17.50

___Narrow Way Character Curriculum & Pearables 1,2, & 3 Volumes SET (listed above) $72.00

___ Personal Help for Boys Text & Workbook $24.95 (Bound in One Book)

Our Hope Chest Series:

___ Volume 1 - Personal Help for Girls $22.50

___ Volume 2 - Preparing Your Hope Chest $22.50

The Quiet Arts Series, <u>Home Economics for Home Schoolers</u>:

___ Level 1 (Ages 6 and up) $18.95
___ Level 2 (Ages 8 and up) $18.95
___ Level 3 (Ages 10 and up) $18.95

___ALL three Levels of Home Economics $45

The Gentleman's Series, <u>Lessons in Responsibility</u>

___ Level 1 (Ages 6 and up) $18.95
___ Level 2 (Ages 8 and up) $18.95

___Subtotal
___ Shipping (Please add $3 for orders under $30. $30 & over please add 10%. Out of U.S. please add 25% of total.)

Name_____

Address_____

City/St/Zip_____

Please mail your purchase order to:

PEARABLES
P.O. Box 1071
Mukilteo, WA 98275

Visit **www.pearables.com** for samples and FREE SHIPPING online.